Redemption from Darkness

Gavin Cross

Copyright © 2022 Gavin Cross
All rights reserved.
ISBN: 9798847741897

No part of this publication may be reproduced, distributed, or transmitted in any form, including photocopying, recording, or other electronic or mechanical methods, without the prior written permission of the author, except in the case of brief quotations embodied in critical reviews and certain other noncommercial uses permitted by copyright law.

Although the author and publisher have made every effort to ensure that the information in this book was correct at press time, the author and publisher do not assume and hereby disclaim any liability to any party for any loss, damage, or disruption caused by errors or omissions, whether such errors or omissions result from negligence, accident, or any other cause.

Dedication

To my Lord and Savior, Jesus Christ, thank you for entrusting me to write this life changing book.

This book is dedicated, with love, to my beautiful loving wife, Dana Cross, who has given me more than I ever wanted and prayed for.

Also, to my beloved sister Crystal Rene' Cross, who is now resting with the Lord.

Thank you, Apostle Onika Brown, for pushing me to birth this. I couldn't have done this without you!

Table of Contents

Introduction: 1

Part 1: Encouragement for times when your faith is weak! 3

Part 2: Encouragement in times when life and faith collide! 7

Part 3: Encouragement when life hits you hard! 16

Part 4: Encouragement to flourish! 25

GAVIN CROSS

Introduction:

This book is for those who may be struggling with their faith. I want you encourage you that your dark seasons will not last forever. God has perfect timing – He is never early, never late. It just takes a little patience and a whole lot of faith but it's worth the wait. Gods' plan is always the best sometimes the process is painful and hard but don't forget that God is silent He's doing something for you. Sometimes God closes doors because it's time to move forward and He knows you won't move unless your circumstances force you to.

You may be thinking about how you're so calculated and you like to know the outcome before things even happen. You feel that you have to protect yourself, but God wants you to trust Him...fully! As you read this, I pray that you are encouraged to keep moving, keep pressing, and believe

God's word for you. You will come out of this!

Part 1:

Encouragement for times when your faith is weak!

1. Bold faith produces uncommon results.
2. If God is all you have, you have all you need.
3. The God I serve is the God who protects and preserves.
4. Until your eyes are set on your Heavenly Father, nothing in this world will ever be enough. No person or thing will ever make you whole or fill that void.
5. The love of Jesus outweighs anything you will ever face.
6. In Christ your past is settled, your present is covered, and your future is secured.
7. The enemy put your bad news in their ears, but watch God announce your good news over the intercom!
8. You may be going through a hard time right now, but keep declaring this, "The hand of God is upon my life."

9. Two lies of the enemy – "you can't; you won't". This is your season remember that.
10. People rejecting you is a sign that God is selecting you.
11. Fill your mind with God's word and you will have no room for the devil's lies.
12. Worship isn't about what we get; worship is about us coming to God to give Him the praise that He is due.
13. You have to stop telling bad spirits good news.
14. A word to the wise: I'm still moving with love; I'm just practicing much more discernment.
15. Worship and worry do not mix.
16. God help me to love like you.

Notes: What are some positive words you can add to this section that you have told yourself lately or that you need to hear?

_____
_____
_____
_____
_____
_____
_____
_____
_____
_____
_____
_____
_____
_____
_____
_____
_____
_____
_____
_____

Part 2:

Encouragement in times when life and faith collide!

1. Somebody, right now, is begging God for the opportunities you have. Don't go to bed depressed. Count your blessings and shake it off.
2. Make no apologies for how you are about to move.
3. When Satan strikes, strike back with the word of God.
4. God never allows pain without a purpose.
5. God will do something in you before He does something through you.
6. Be strong now, it will get better. It may be stormy now, but it can't rain forever.
7. God work in me through your word today. Fill my mind with your truth and hope.
8. The reason you haven't lost your mind is because God is still in control.
9. You belong to God. You are special, you are chosen, you are enough!

10. The best part about getting back on your feet is knowing who not to walk with again.
11. Struggling, does not mean failing.
12. Stop being the go-to person for people you can't go to.
13. Watch people who keep switching sides. They are more interested in "winning" than they are in "you".
14. Life is fragile; handle it with prayer.
15. Your story is defined by Jesus, not by brokenness.
16. God is turning things around to bless you in a major way!
17. No matter how many mistakes you make or how slow you progress, you are still way ahead of everyone who isn't trying.
18. It's not the load that weighs you down, it's the way you carry it.
19. Don't you dare shrink yourself for someone else's comfort. Do not become small for people who refuse to grow.

20. Jesus, you are my King, my savior, and my friend. Draw near to me as I draw near to you.
21. Every gift, talent, and ability that God put in you is to impact others.
22. When you don't move like everyone else, it bothers people.
23. Jesus will love you when no one else will.
24. God is far more concerned with your *availability* than He is with your *ability*.
25. They're judging because you keep starting over; I'm clapping because you never gave up!
26. Don't be afraid to start at the bottom. There's a lot of people pretending to be at the top.
27. Let go of things that make you feel dead. Life is worth living.
28. Consistency doesn't mean never messing up; it means never giving up.

29. Don't let sins that were committed against you produce sin in you.
30. God didn't give you the gift for you; it isn't to make you great. The gift was given so Gods generosity can flow through you.
31. Move in grace, love, gratitude, and most of all integrity.
32. Be inspired to live free.
33. Stop comparing yourself to other people. The expectation, for you, different.
34. Don't give up on your purpose because things are getting a little harder. Keep praying until things fall into place.
35. The Holy Spirit doesn't make me better than you; it makes me better than me.
36. God is greater than the highs and lows of life.
37. The longer you entertain what's not of God, the longer you postpone what is.

38. They laughed at your process, but you will laugh in your promise!
39. Nobody watches you harder than the people that don't like you…give them something to see.
40. I stopped explaining myself when I realize people only understood things from their level of perception.
41. Removing yourself, instead of returning negative energy, is growth.
42. Love God and love people. We cannot do one without the other.
43. Never allow the enemy to make you quit.
44. Even if God says no or not yet will you still serve Him?
45. The circumstances that surround you are surrounded by a God who is greater than any circumstance.
46. Staying in your comfort zone will cause you to forfeit what

God has for you because of familiarity.
47. Faith is the in-between space. It is stepping out when you don't see the steps and turning knobs where there are no keys.
48. God answers all prayers in one of three ways: yes, because you deserve it. No, because you deserve better, and not yet, because the best is yet to come.
49. They can take their best shot, but you'll still come out on top.
50. I don't want anybody around me with a jealous heart or a hateful soul.
51. Refine, refocus, restore, renew…live again.
52. The blessed don't beef with the miserable.
53. Until you are at peace with yourself, and God, you can never experience peace with anyone.
54. You're coming out of the stronger, wiser, and better than ever!

55. When your heart is pure and true God has a way of making sure that everything works out in your favor.
56. Work on things people can't take away from you – your character, personality, inner peace, and your entire being.
57. Don't use your energy to worry. Use your energy to believe, create, grow, and heal.
58. People will judge you. They will make negative comments. They waste time talking about others while you utilize your time building your legacy. Let them watch while you win.

Notes: What are some positive words you can add to this section that you have told yourself lately or that you need to hear?

Part 3:

Encouragement when life hits you hard!

1. The only person you can change is yourself. If others change because of your actions or words, it's because they ultimately choose to do so.
2. When God approves your purpose, you don't need a cosigner to walk in it.
3. They laughed at your process, but you will laugh in your promise.
4. The storm you're in is temporary, but the strength you'll gain from it is everlasting.
5. Your current situation is not your destination. God has more for you!
6. If you never heal from what hurt, you you'll bleed on people who never cut you.
7. You can't grow with people who don't like how growth looks on you.
8. Everyone can't change the world, but everyone can change their world.

9. The key to overcoming big problems is to grow yourself until the problems get small.
10. We don't need to be fearless to be bold. We just need to stop letting fear paralyze us.
11. When the devil plays checkers against you, God plays chess against Him.
12. Love pouring out of you is evidence that God is pouring into you.
13. When everything around you seems out of control, that is the perfect time to elevate your standards.
14. If your faith can move mountains, then why are your mountains still there?
15. If you're serious about change, you have to go through uncomfortable situations. Stop trying to dodge the process; it's how you grow.
16. Take responsibility for your feelings, and actions, no matter who or what triggered them.

17. If you are unwilling to face the pain, you will continue to live in it.
18. Mistreating people, then avoiding communication, is not protecting your peace; it's avoiding accountability.
19. Growth is painful, but nothing is more painful than staying in a place you don't belong.
20. God can't do a new thing if you continue to look backwards.
21. Only humility can get you out of what pride get you into.
22. There is no way God brought you this far to watch you fail.
23. You will never be more popular, in this world, than you are when you are in the midst of self-destruction.
24. Don't cry over the past; it's gone. Don't stress about the future; it hasn't arrived. Live in the present and make it beautiful.
25. Even a negative situation holds the potential to produce a positive purpose / outcome.

26. They won't realize how big of a part you play until you are not playing it anymore.
27. Stop giving CPR to dead situations.
28. Learn to heal without venting to everyone.
29. Stop searching for light and dim people.
30. When God doesn't have your attention, He will disturb what does.
31. Every blessing that is formed for me shall prosper!
32. Not doing them how they did you is what's keeping your blessings coming.
33. Don't ruin other people's happiness just because you can't find your own.
34. Jesus sat with sinners, but He didn't sin with Him.
35. God is taking you to a place you've never been before so we must trust Him even when we can't understand what He's doing.

36. Don't worry about people copying you. The next move can't happen until you make yours.
37. You have to learn to break generational curses without a support of those who passed them on.
38. Pain will teach you a lesson that pride won't let you learn.
39. Shutting down instead of communicating is just as toxic as arguing.
40. Sometimes God won't let you come up until every snake in your circle is gone.
41. You can't be an adult and continue to blame your actions on your zodiac sign.
42. People don't want to know the truth; they want to be comfortable.
43. Whoever is trying to bring you down is already below you.
44. Treating people right is better than posting Bible verses, every day, that you don't practice.

45. Be careful who you listen to; critics run with critics, and critics run their mouths.
46. God will bring you out of situations that you got yourself into, and He won't hold it against you.
47. God won't give you what was intended for someone else. Stop comparing your season to someone else's.
48. Obstacles aren't limitations. They're building blocks to create the toughness required to maintain your next level.
49. The people you choose to associate with will either blur your vision or clarify it.
50. Following God will lead you to a place where your enemies will have to watch you walk in your blessings.
51. Fix your attention on God. You'll be changed from the inside out. God brings the best out of you and develops a well-formed maturity in you.

52. Never trust your fears; they don't know your strength.
53. Repentance is not an apology, it's an act of obedience, a change of mind, attitude, and behavior empowered by the Holy Spirit.
54. God is giving you the strength to defeat what's in front of you.
55. Appreciate where you are in your journey, even if it's not where you want to be. Every season serves a purpose.
56. Vibrate so faithfully and positively that toxic people want to run with you or run away from you.
57. Don't use your energy to worry. Use your energy to believe, create, grow, and heal.
58. People will judge you. They will make negative comments. They waste time talking about others while you utilize your time building your legacy. Let them watch while you win.

Notes: What are some positive words you can add to this section that you have told yourself lately or that you need to hear?

_____
_____
_____
_____
_____
_____
_____
_____
_____
_____
_____
_____
_____
_____
_____
_____
_____
_____

Part 4:

Encouragement to flourish!

1. When you die to your former self that's when you will begin to live.
2. Stop shrinking yourself to fit into areas you've outgrown.
3. If it's pulling you away from God, it's not from God.
4. God has an invested interest in you!
5. A bad attitude can literally block love, blessings, and destiny from finding you. Don't be the reason you don't succeed.
6. Darkness cannot drive out darkness; only light can do that.
7. Don't limit yourself from the limitless God we serve.
8. Everybody is not built like you so never expect the same in return.
9. You can be overlooked, talked about, plotted against, and still come out on top.
10. When your eyes are on God, the size of your Goliath doesn't matter.

11. Let God in today. Stop trying to control everything or everything will control you.
12. Plans…private moves…silent life. Lowkey - pray loud!
13. If you're not trying to change the broken things in your life, you're choosing to keep them. Remember that!
14. If you want to see what's next in your life, release your past. You have to let it go in order to move forward.
15. Ignorance is not an excuse for your actions.
16. You may have been knocked down, but get back up again. You can do this. God will strengthen you for the journey. Don't ever give up!
17. Every family has a person that will break the chain of poverty. May you be that blessing to your family.
18. Your blessings will far outweigh the battle you are going through.

19. Sometimes God's answer is difficult to hear because our minds are already made up.
20. Everything is not the devil; sometimes it's your decision.
21. Some people only talk about you because they lost the privilege to talk to you.
22. Sometimes people haven't apologized because they're ashamed. Forgive them anyway. Sometimes you have to be OK without an apology.
23. Walking with God is a game changing strategy.
24. Denying God with your words is no more offensive than proclaiming Him with your words while denying Him with your actions.
25. Don't get in the way of your own purpose.
26. Even when it doesn't work, God is still working things out.

27. You get tested the most when it's time for you to elevate. Don't break.
28. Keep trusting, even when you don't see that better is coming.
29. Refusing the guidance of the Holy Spirit is like driving your car blindfolded while wearing earplugs.
30. You live your best life when you invite God into it.
31. May you have the courage to break the patterns, in your life, that are no longer serving you.
32. Spring clean your soul. What used to work for you may not be working because you have evolved.
33. Replace your negative self-talk with "I am learning and growing. I am proud of myself for trying. I am worthy and good enough!"
34. Make sure the people you allow around you have love for you.

Notes: What are some positive words you can add to this section that you have told yourself lately or that you need to hear?

Made in United States
Orlando, FL
26 August 2022